T0196691

Prayer
or Communication
with God

Prayer
or Communication
with God

Veronica O' Connor

authorHOUSE®

AuthorHouse™
1663 Liberty Drive
Bloomington, IN 47403
www.authorhouse.com
Phone: 1-800-839-8640

© *2011 by Veronica O' Connor. All rights reserved.*

No part of this book may be reproduced, stored in a retrieval system, or transmitted by any means without the written permission of the author.

First published by AuthorHouse   12/30/2011

ISBN: 978-1-4685-3580-8 (sc)
ISBN: 978-1-4685-3579-2 (ebk)

Library of Congress Control Number: 2011963435

Printed in the United States of America

Any people depicted in stock imagery provided by Thinkstock are models, and such images are being used for illustrative purposes only.
Certain stock imagery © Thinkstock.

This book is printed on acid-free paper.

Because of the dynamic nature of the Internet, any web addresses or links contained in this book may have changed since publication and may no longer be valid. The views expressed in this work are solely those of the author and do not necessarily reflect the views of the publisher, and the publisher hereby disclaims any responsibility for them.

Contents

Prayer or Communication with God

Introduction...*vii*

Prayer *1*

What is prayer?...*5*

Why pray?...*9*

Who executes prayer? *11*

To whom should we pray?..*15*

When and where should we pray? *17*

How should we pray *21*

What should we pray for?...*25*

The results of prayer...*29*

Channels through which God responds......................*33*

Individual Prayers *37*

References...*73*

Introduction

I was brought up to understand that if I wanted something, I needed to ask for it. After I asked, sometimes my request was granted, and sometimes it was not. When I was dealing with my parents, there were times when I received an immediate response; when I received no response, that meant I needed to reconsider what I was asking for—or quit asking at all.

I grew up to accept Jesus Christ as my Lord and Savior. According to 1 John 3:1, "behold what manner of love the father hath bestowed upon us that we should be called the sons of God." God was my spiritual parent, facilitating my need for communication with Him, which is done through prayer.

This book covers all aspects of communication with God, from the definition of prayer to how, when, why, and where to pray. It concludes with a discussion of the results of prayer followed by some specific prayers that can be used in difficult situations.

Prayer

***Prayer:** a spoken or unspoken address to God, a deity, or a saint. It may express praise, thanksgiving, or confession, or it may request help for something such as everyday activities or someone's well-being.*

***Communication:** the exchange of information between people, e.g. by means of speaking, writing, or using a common system of signs or behavior.*

Encarta English Dictionary

The word prayer is mentioned 114 times in the King James Bible. The Bible places a great focus on prayer because man is connected to God, and there must be a channel through which intimacy, a bond of sweet fellowship, is maintained between them.

When God created Adam and Eve, the first humans, He placed them in the Garden of Eden. In the cool of the day, God would go down to the garden to communicate and have fellowship with them. Genesis 3:8-10 states that one day when God went down as he usually did, Adam and

Eve hid themselves from Him, so God called Adam, asking where he was. Adam realized that he had disobeyed God, so he tried to cast blame on Eve. Since then, it has been man's obligation to seek God and to reestablish that connection with Him through prayer.

Prayer is the most powerful channel of communication. People of faith depend immensely on prayer because it's a vital weapon in the hands of all believers. Through this medium they find many ways to confront their problems. Through prayer they connect with themselves and with the heavenly host. They achieve peace of mind and self-acceptance, becoming physically, spiritually, and emotionally stronger and thereby gaining the courage to continue living another day. It's no coincidence that when someone is facing a difficult situation, a friend or loved one often will offer some form of consolation and end by saying, "I will pray for you," "I will remember you in my prayers," or, "My prayers are with you."

The ritual of prayer has been a fixed part of my thought process since my childhood days, when I was as young as four. I still remember that just before my mother tucked my siblings and me into bed, I would hear her voice drift in from the next room:

"Did you read your Bible? Remember to say your prayers before you go to sleep!"

For a child, of course, saying a prayer every night is like reciting a nursery rhyme. But it brings comfort and satisfaction to a young heart.

As for my siblings and I, our prayer was simple and ritualistic. We knelt with hands clasped and eyes closed and recited the prayer hastily, without a pause. We were not concerned about the meaning of each line of the prayer:

Gentle Jesus, meek and mild,
look upon a little child,
pity my simplicity,
suffer me to come to thee,
Amen.

We would end the prayer by saying, "Good night, Jesus. Good night, Mother. Good night, Daddy."

At five o'clock each morning, in the cool hills of Point Hill, Jamaica, everyone in my family would be awakened by the *cock-a-doodle-doo* of roosters in the backyard and birds chirping in the giant fig tree by our house. This high-pitched, continuous sound would work its way into our ears even as we snuggled deeper under our covers; the birds' voices echoed through the air like a choir chanting praises to God most high, signaling that it was time for the family to rise to face another new day. At this point we offered another prayer, thanking God for our good night's sleep and requesting His continuous blessing throughout the day. Respect for the ritual of prayer was instilled in us quite early, and the meaning of prayer was not hard to understand. We understood that when we prayed, we were simply talking to God and expecting Him to listen to our requests.

What is prayer?

The almighty God created humans with a unique need for some sort of connection to the Divine Host. We can activate this connection through regular prayer and worship.

Prayer is basic communication or dialogue with the Supreme Being, He who rules the universe and is the creator of human life.

When the term *Supreme Being* is mentioned to children, they interpret it to mean *God*; little children might envision some version of "Gentle Jesus, meek and mild." As children blossom into young adults, however, they develop a more mature perception of God and the meaning of prayer. With this new, multifaceted understanding of God, they can read the scriptures and find other revelations of Him:

God as king: the one who rules the world with great authority and pride. "And he shall reign over the house of Jacob forever, and of his kingdom there shall be no end" (Luke 1:33).

God as savior: the only one capable of saving humans from sin. "And thou shall call his name Jesus for he shall save his people from their sins" (Matt. 1:22).

God as redeemer: "He gave his life as a sacrifice to redeem us back to righteousness" (Titus 2:14).

God as friend: "Greater love hath no man than this that a man lay down his life for his friend" (John 15:13).

God as comforter: "Blessed be God . . . who comforts us in all our tribulation that we may be able to comfort them which are in trouble" (2 Cor. 1:3-4).

God is also father to the fatherless and a present help in times of trouble—something many children need today. For some reason, a large percentage of fathers are failing to fulfill their responsibilities to their children. A vast number of women, married and unmarried, have been neglected by their companions and left with the burden of raising their children alone. These single-parent families can find themselves in dire need of assistance. But the loving God, who is motivated by prayer, always provides help for the fatherless and the helpless.

He is also known as the **God of love and mercies**, yet the Bible also tells us He can be a **God of vengeance or consuming fire**. This contradicting view forces us away from childlike prayer to a wider and more meaningful conversation with God. Then we find that as individuals who believe and live in prayer, we have stronger faith and live a more productive and fulfilling life.

Prayer is like an electrical cord through which humanity connects to God when there is the need for supernatural intervention. At times we feel lost and disconnected from God; prayer is the channel through which we keep our ongoing relationship with Him alive.

Through prayer we recognize that we are helpless and must succumb to a divine force that is more powerful than we are. On April 15, 1912, the "unsinkable" Titanic plunged mercilessly into the hungry sea. I can almost hear those hundreds of desperate souls singing "Nearer, My God, to Thee" at the top of their voices while others helplessly succumb to the divine powers, uttering their last prayer of comfort and surrender: "Have mercy on me, oh God."

Prayer is universal. In every culture in every corner of the world, there are moments set aside to incorporate prayer into daily life. Lindsey Roberts, [wife of Richard Roberts, television evangelist] has mentioned that her television ministry receives more than two thousand prayer requests a day. No wonder television evangelist Joel Osteen said, "A day without prayer is a day without a blessing; a life without prayer is a life without power."

Prayer to God results in great satisfaction of the soul. It makes you feel complete, accepted in the supernatural realm.

Prayer can take many forms—verbal or nonverbal, complex or simple. Often I'll hear believers begin their prayer with phrases like "Dear Lord our God, the great and almighty one" or "Oh Jesus, love divine, supreme God, lover of my soul, I pray to you this moment." Other times the prayer can be short but to the point—acknowledging God for who He is, thanking Him for present blessings, and then requesting His guidance for the future or His attendance to some immediate, personal needs.

Prayer can also be lengthy, depending on the individual and the purpose of the prayer. Some people take time to address the awesomeness of God using a variety of descriptive words like *glorious, gracious, wonderful, supreme, divine, omnipotent*—the list goes on and on.

An individual can also take prayer as an opportunity to recommit himself, acknowledging that he is unworthy and undeserving of God's love, asking for forgiveness of his sins, and finally requesting grace and mercy to continue living. If there is a specific problem lying heavily on his heart, this would be the time to mention it and perhaps repeat it over and over again. Before ending, he usually says thanks in advance for the answered prayer, with the assurance that his request will be granted. In conclusion, he might endorse the prayer by saying, "Amen," "Halleluiah," or, "In the name of Jesus."

Prayer often takes a nonverbal form when someone is overcome by deep emotions; she might groan, sigh, cry, look up to the sky, clasp her hands with her eyes closed, or simply remain silent and stay in deep meditation for a while. All of this spurs spiritual communication with God as that intense, electrifying power begins to stir within her body, allowing her to be aware of God's presence and resulting in deep satisfaction.

Sometimes people prefer to write down their prayer to be read by themselves or others. Some individuals go so far as to secretly lay their written prayer on a church altar, trusting that a spiritual leader will read it and petition God on their behalf, or that an angel will convey the request to heaven and then return with God's answer. It's not unusual to see Oral Roberts or other television preachers with piles of prayer requests stacked on a nearby table; they pray over these requests, and through their faith, the writers of these requests are healed of whatever ailments they have.

Why pray?

Genesis 1:27 states, "so God created man in his own image, in the image of God created him, male and female . . ."

Humans were created of God, by God, and for God:

Of God—because we were fashioned after His own image. We are expected to have things in common with God. He prays, so we should pray. He worships and performs good deeds, so we are expected to do likewise.

By God—because Genesis 2:7 states that the Lord God formed man of the dust of the earth and breathed into his nostrils the breath of life. By this we know that our earthly structure contains God's precious breath—hence our connection with Him.

For God—because Ecclesiastes 12:13 states that we are to fear God and keep His commandments—that this is the whole duty of man.

In order for us to fear God and keep His commandments, we must be in continuous communication with God through Jesus, His son. We must read His word in the holy book, a practice that should be reinforced on a regular basis. As replicas of God Himself, carved by His divine hands and shaped in His likeness, we must maintain interaction with Him through prayer. After all, we are His children, so we must adopt His principles, just as Jesus did. Before His crucifixion, Jesus prayed, "Father, if thou be willing, remove this cup from me, nevertheless not my will but thine be done" (Luke 22:42).

He also told His disciples to pray so that they would not enter into temptation (Luke 22:40). Hearing this advice from Jesus himself gives us a good reason to pray and reminds us that a life without prayer is an open gateway for the enemy to succeed. Therefore we should pray just as our Lord and master does.

Isn't this another valid cause to engage in daily prayer throughout the year?

Who executes prayer?

Daily prayer is critical for anyone who believes in the divine creator, the God of heaven in combination with His extended spirit that came to earth, took human form, and dwelled among us. He has been called by many names, among them *Jesus, Emmanuel, the Prince of Peace*, and *the Almighty*.

Believers in God include religious ministers, pastors, evangelists, deacons, auxiliary church leaders, and church members and even non-members. But all of them find it vital to pray on a daily basis.

Jesus Himself followed this ritual when He woke up early in the morning, went to a solitary place, and prayed (Mark 1:35). In Matthew 6:9, He became the perfect example of faith in action, showing the disciples how to pray by saying, "After this manner therefore pray ye:"

> *Our Father which art in heaven,*
> *hallowed be thy name.*
> *thy kingdom come.*
> *thy will be done*
> *in earth, as it is in heaven.*
> *Give us this day our daily bread.*

> *And forgive us our debts,*
> *as we forgive our debtors.*
> *And lead us not into temptation,*
> *but deliver us from evil:*
> *for thine is the kingdom, and the power, and the glory,*
> *for ever. Amen.*

In the early 1970s, I knew a police officer in Kingston, Jamaica. He was also a prominent man of God, and on many occasions I saw and heard him pray in a manner that sent many others to prayer on bended knee.

Each time he prayed, he cried like a baby, causing his congregation to be moved by heartfelt emotion. It was also said that whenever he was on police duty and apprehended someone for a minor infraction, he would command the person to kneel and pray for forgiveness and then send him on his way, instructing him to find a church where he could worship. He was known to many as "the weeping policeman," but he should have been dubbed "the praying mantis." He was never afraid to use the weapon of prayer on or off duty; in fact, when his colleagues were confronted with a difficult case, he would be the first one to say, "Let's take it to the Lord in prayer."

President of the United State, [Barack Obama] saw prayer as great importance when he asked Pastor Rick Warren to pray at the 2009 Presidential inauguration. This gave rise to some controversy, as numerous citizens questioned whether the pastor was an appropriate choice for this occasion. The fact is, prayer is not the tool of any special group or person. Whoever feels the need to exercise his faith in prayer is welcome to do so, whether he is rich or poor, black or white, good or bad. "This poor man cried and

the Lord heard him and saved him out of all his troubles"
(Ps. 34:6)

Even popular secular figures like Oprah Winfrey can
model a prayerful life. In announcing that her twenty-fifth
season would be her last, she told her viewers she had come
to that decision "after much prayer and months of careful
thought."

When we communicate with our Lord God, we also
look for some form of acknowledgement from Him.
Therefore as we pray, we should not only focus on what we
are saying, but we also should listen for the voice of God.
Sometimes He grants an immediate response; other times,
it takes hours, days, months, or even years before a prayer
is answered. "And the Lord God appeared to Solomon
by night and said unto him, I have heard thy prayer and
have chosen this place to myself for a house of sacrifice" (2
Chron. 7:12).

As slaves of the Egyptian pharaoh, the children of Israel
prayed and cried to God daily. God heard their cries, but it
was years before He took action. "And the Lord said, I have
surely seen the affliction of my people . . . and have heard
their cry . . . And I am come down to deliver them out of
the hand of the Egyptians and to bring them up out of that
land unto a good land . . . flowing with milk and honey"
(Exod. 3:7-8).

I have known my parents to be prayer warriors. During
my childhood in Jamaica, things were extremely rough for
my mother, in particular. She suffered under great financial
strain, and one of her means of survival was to pray daily; as
a result, our "daily bread" was supplied in amounts sufficient
to feed a family of twelve adults and children.

There were days when we children would arrive home
from school at 4:30 p.m. to find that there was nothing

in the kitchen to make a meal for the family. We lived deep in the rural area of the island, without running water, electricity, and other modern facilities, so not only did we often lack provisions for supper, but sometimes there was little water in the jar and no wood to make a fire. But our mother knew the effectiveness of good communication with her God. She would turn her eyes to the sky and ask, "Lord, what's for dinner tonight?" By six o'clock her prayer would be answered, and our family was able to give thanks for another day's meal, provisions given by good neighbors, friends, or distant relatives willing to share.

Every day at noon, a plane would fly across the sky over our home. When Mother saw that plane she would stop what she was doing and again lift her eyes to the sky, communicating with her God. "Lord," she would ask, "when will I be able to fly in one of those planes?" Ten years later, her prayers were answered; she traveled to and from the United States and Canada on numerous occasions to visit with relatives and friends.

My stepfather prayed loud and long. At six o'clock every morning he would begin his prayer: "Lord, remember me when Thou comest into thy kingdom. Lord, remember my children at home and abroad. Lord, remember my relatives and friends. Lord, touch my church brothers and sisters, from the pastor right down to the least member. Lord, touch the leaders of the country; unite everyone's heart together and let them rule your people according to your will. Lord, remember the sick and the lame. Lord, remember the haves and the have-nots . . ." The prayer would go on and on as my stepfather called the names of different people until he seemed to run out of words. By then he would have covered everyone, including the fowl of the air, the beasts of the field, and the fish of the sea.

To whom should we pray?

According to Luke 11:2, when we pray, we should say, "Our Father, which art in heaven, hallowed be thy name." In directing our prayers, we Christians recognize no alternatives. We believe in Jesus Christ, son of God, so whenever we pray, the prayer should be directed to the almighty God who is our father in heaven.

Jesus was that king who came down from heaven, becoming a baby born of the virgin so that He could grow up as a typical child. When Jesus was born in Bethlehem of Judea, three wise men went searching for Him, eventually finding Him with His mother (Matt. 2:11). Immediately they bowed down and prayed, worshipping their new king, Jesus.

During His crucifixion, Jesus was placed between two thieves, one of whom prayed to Jesus, saying, "Lord, remember me when thou comest into thy kingdom" (Luke 23:42). Immediately, the thief got a response: Jesus assured him that he would be with Him in paradise that very day. The thief's prayer was answered.

When King David died and his son Solomon took over his reign, Solomon felt inadequate and unskilled to rule such a great nation. According to 1 Kings 3:9, he prayed for God to give him an understanding heart to judge the people, so that he might discern between good and evil. History revealed that King Solomon ruled with wisdom, justice, and dignity because he asked God through prayer to direct his leadership.

In some religions, all prayer is directed to God, the supreme one who creates heaven and earth; in others, prayer is directed to Holy Mary, mother of God, and sometimes to other holy saints. Adherents to some other religions worship or pray to the cow, the moon, the sun, or some other form of god. However, we read in Isaiah 44:2-6 of "the Lord that made thee and formed thee from the womb . . ." and that "I am the first and I am the last; and beside me there is no God."

I think the fair conclusion would be that if prayer is offered, the focus should be on the Lord God only. Since the scriptures dictate to whom we should pray, we should adhere to that rule accordingly, praying to the God of the universe, the God of all flesh.

When and where should we pray?

We pray when we have something to say to God. We can express our thoughts, feelings, and fears to Him or just unload our burdens on Him as we would with a dear friend. The more we communicate with our friends, relatives, or companion, the more effective our relationship with them becomes. In Luke 18:1, Jesus explains in a parable that we should pray always and not lose heart.

The Bible offers no written rules about when or where to pray. We may pray at our convenience, but generally we should do it as often as possible. In Psalm 5:3, David says, "My voice shalt thou hear in the morning, oh Lord, in the morning will I direct my prayer unto thee." Then in Psalm 55:17, he vows to pray and cry aloud morning, evening, and noon, knowing that the Lord shall hear his voice.

It would be so appropriate to begin each morning as David did, with a prayer to God, for His love is new every morning. We see that renewal in the splendor of the rising sun as it ascends from the horizon and illuminates the room, and in our own vigorous stretch and yawn as the spirit reconnects with the body after a long night's sleep.

Life continues with another new day, and so do God's blessings.

Once we start the activities of daily living, time goes by quickly with the hustle and bustle of our various chores at home or work. Before we know it, it's noon, and David advises more communication with God.

I remember that during primary school, after a long, hectic morning, we children would become anxious to hear the lunch bell ring so we could rush out for a meal. Before exiting the classroom, however, we had to say grace. This would be the prayer for the lower grades:

> *God is good, God is great.*
> *Let us thank Him for our food.*
> *Amen.*

The upper grades would pray in the form of a song, which went like this:

> *Thank you for the world so sweet.*
> *Thank you for the food we eat.*
> *Thank you for the birds that sing.*
> *Thank you, God, for everything.*
> *Amen.*

Our day seems to end in no time, as we are tired and physically drained from work or play. The evening sun sets in the west, and it's time for the body to be refueled and rejuvenated; we are summoned to rest because another day is promised us. And again, David encourages us to pray. Even Daniel knelt three times a day to pray and give thanks to his God (Dan. 6:10).

It is good to be in constant communication with God, in good times and in bad times. Jesus and the disciples were out sailing when a great storm overtook them. Frightened and panicking, the disciples woke Jesus, who was asleep in one corner of the boat, asking Him if He didn't care that they were about to perish. Jesus got up and spoke to the wind, commanding it to be still. In response to the mighty creator, the wind and the waves became still (Mark 4:35-40).

Good, effective communication will activate our fear of the Lord. As David says in Psalm 25:14, "The secrets of the Lord are with them that fear him and he will show them his covenant."

Whether we are at home, in our cars, at work, or simply caught up in the frenzy of daily life, we should always find a special moment to lift our thoughts in communication with the supreme God of our soul.

Churches have selected areas where worshippers can kneel or stand before the Lord their creator. This is known as the altar, usually built in front of the pulpit. Some schools or universities provide a separate area, often called a "quiet room" or "meditation room," where people of faith can take a few minutes to commune with their God. In places like hospitals, nursing homes, or hospice centers, there is usually a chapel or family room where relatives, friends, or well-wishers can exercise their faith through worship or offer a prayer for their loved ones.

It is widely practiced in North American culture that sometime after a child is born; he is taken to the chapel or church to be dedicated. The dedication ceremony can take many different forms, but it always includes prayer.

When someone is near death, with only a few days or hours left, a priest is often called to the home or hospital to perform the "last rights," a final prayer offered for the beloved in the room or at the bedside. As David says in Psalm 63:5-6, "my mouth shall praise thee with joyful lips, when I remember thee upon my bed and meditate on thee in the night watch."

Prayer should be used as the first approach to every situation in life, not as a last resort. There are individuals who make prayer part of their daily routine, never performing an activity without first praying. If success is the end result, those individuals know it was the will of God.

There are those who use prayer as a last resort; that is, when they are down and out, having exhausted every other source without success, their last option is to try prayer.

There are others who use prayer as an occasional activity. Some visit church twice a year, at Christmas and Easter, to say a prayer. Some visit regularly, just to be sheltered under the prayers of others. Others visit for special ceremonies like weddings, funerals, or graduations. Some of these patrons are visiting church for the first time to say a prayer or listen to someone else pray.

How to pray

When the three wise men found baby Jesus in the manger, they all bowed and worshipped Him (Matt. 2:11). In Psalm 95:6 David says, "Oh come let us worship and bow down; let us kneel before the Lord our maker."

Worshippers today have many different ways and forms of praying. Some kneel, bow their heads, and close their eyes; some stand with clasped hands; others stand motionless and silent for a minute or two.

Some believers recognize the cross as a means of communication with God, kissing the cross or touching their forehead, chest, and shoulders to symbolize the cross. By doing this they show gratitude for God's blessings and acknowledge the Lord's presence.

There are some believers who bow down and kiss the earth as a form of reverence, accepting the fact that they were created from the dust of the earth. Whatever form of prayer is most comfortable for you, or whatever form is accepted within your congregation, by all means use it.

When I was a child of God growing up under the divine ministerial leaders, prayer was the main focus of my faith. Any worship service would commence with a prayer, more prayers would be offered two or three times during the service, and finally the service would climax with yet another soul-searching prayer. Believers would be on their knees for hours, praying loud and long, their prayers accompanied by loud cries and hallowing of the name of Jesus. Hearing them, I often would wonder, "How far away is this God? Is He deaf? Is He ignoring His people? Or is He punishing them for their sins?" As I got older and wiser, however, I came to realize that as people engage in sincere prayer, they begin to sense the presence of God, and their emotions manifest themselves in different ways.

Some preachers prefer to have their followers form lines so the preachers can pray over them and anoint them with olive oil. The trend with most television preachers today is to keep small pieces of material or even small vials of holy water which they pray over and then send to their believers as a means of contact. Some ask their viewers to reach toward the television or even touch the screen as a prayer is offered up; others ask that while prayer is in progress, viewers touch an area of the body that needs healing. Often when I'm engaged in prayer at home, I find it very comfortable and effective to lie on my bed and quietly commune with my God. There are times when my friends and I call each other to talk about our concerns, and we will pray for each other right over the phone.

Some churches send their members from house to house to have a prayer session with believers and nonbelievers. During the visit they will discuss Bible passages and offer a prayer for the individual.

It was part of Jamaican culture in the early 1960s that women were forbidden to pray with uncovered heads; if a woman was praying or being prayed for, she would wear some form of covering on her head. Men, however, could not pray with a covered head; if they entered a church or synagogue, they were expected to remove their hat. This was a form of reverence to the almighty God.

Culture and tradition seem to change with the time. Now it's common to see both women and men praying with or without a covering on their heads.

What should we pray for?

From what I've seen and experienced, I realize that the need for prayer is enormous. People are confused, perplexed, and feel pressured from every side. As a result, they hunger and thirst for spiritual satisfaction, relying on prayer for basically every concern. What should we pray for?

We should pray for everything—from a pin to an anchor, for things present or future. I remember that when I bought my first car and took it home, I sat in it and prayed, giving thanks for my accomplishment. That car served my family well, and I never had an accident.

We should pray for every activity we perform, whether it is pleasant or unpleasant. During the course of our work, we sometimes are required to perform activities that are unpleasant or dangerous, but because they are our job, they have to be done. We should pray constantly for our protection at work.

We should pray for all the occupants of Mother Earth, whether they live in the sea or on land. This includes humans, animals, birds, fish, and insects.

We should pray for everything that occupies space. Whether it controls the day or the night. Altogether our heavenly Father provides everything for the benefit of mankind.

We should pray for our daily needs:

Food is essential for survival. A single day without food has ill effect on our health, so we should pray for every meal we need and offer thanksgiving for every meal we consume. The children of Israel had a fresh supply of bread from heaven daily (Exod. 16:4).

Clothing is also a daily essential. The elements don't always treat our bodies kindly, so we need clothing to protect our skin from the heat and the cold. According to Genesis 3:7, when Adam and Eve realized that they were naked, they sewed fig leaves together to clothe themselves.

Shelter is another daily need that we should pray for. Fortunately, we were not created like the animals, who can withstand the rain, sun, and snow bearing down on their bodies. Especially when night comes, we look forward to going home to bond with our families and feel safe from the unknown. The day after I bought my new home, I invited my brethren over for a lovely prayer meeting to offer praise and thanks to God before I moved in.

We should pray for our families, neighbors, and friends. A home without prayer is a failing home. Parents treat their children with contempt; children retaliate by being disrespectful, ungrateful, self-centered, and cheap. Spouses are unfaithful to one another and may be physically or verbally abusive to each other. When a family refuses to communicate with God, they allow all kinds of negative forces to thrive in their homes. These negative forces affect spouses, children, and even pets, causing division among family members.

In the greater community, neighbors should be Good Samaritans. For a community to be at peace and a model of good morals and values, each individual must pray earnestly for his neighbors. It is true that "no man is an island," because God created us with the need for each other; that's why we have friends, neighbors, and families. However for our friends to remain loyal and true, we need to pray constantly for them. James 5:16-17 advises us to confess our faults to one another and pray for one another so that we may be healed. It goes on to say that the effectual, fervent prayer of a righteous man is very powerful.

We should pray for our country's leaders and all those who serve with authority. It is recommended in 1 Timothy 2:1-3 that we offer supplications, prayers, intercessions, and thanks for all leaders, including kings and others in authority, that they lead quiet, peaceful lives of godliness and reverence.

We should pray for health and strength. "Beloved, I wish above all things that thou mayest prosper and be in health, even as thy soul prospereth" (3 John 1:2). Humans are not immune to all the diseases that plague the earth, so Christ provided the opportunity for man to be healed of whatever disease he encounters. This He made possible through the shedding of His blood, so when we engage in prayer and fasting to Him, His healing powers are activated and we are healed of diseases. He also gave physicians the wisdom and knowledge to use medication appropriately to eliminate disease from the body. John thought that good health was a vital aspect of living; that's why he wished above anything else that his fellow men be in good health.

We should pray for our finances. Money was invented for the exchange of goods and services and for the repayment of debts. It is to be spent wisely and used for purposes that fairly build and promote the nation's prosperity. It is okay to pursue and possess some money; however, the Bible states that the love of money is the root of all evil. We are reminded in 1 Timothy 6:10 that some have strayed from the faith while coveting money, piercing themselves through with many sorrows. Therefore, we should pray that God gives us the wisdom to handle our finances with care so that His glory will be made manifest.

We should pray for the protection of our dwelling place. It does not surprise me when I enter someone's home and see some form of plaque hanging on the walls with the caption "My Kitchen Prayer" or "My Bathroom Prayer." Because Satan is cunning, it would be wise to have a prayer for every single room in the house so that whenever you enter a room, whether to work, play, or relax, your spirit will freely recognize the presence of the Lord.

The results of prayer

We must be disciplined in our prayer to get good results from it. "If my people, which are called by my name, shall humble themselves and pray and seek my face and turn from their wicked ways; then will I hear from heaven and will forgive their sin and heal their land" (2 Chron. 7:14). Through the power of prayer, believers have experienced a variety of great results:

Sins have been forgiven. Humans are born and by nature inherit sin. Our relatives, friends, or neighbors can say they forgive us for our sins, but the only effective forgiveness comes from God himself. With confidence that our sins are forgiven, we can then move forward and lead a more productive life.

Spirits have been uplifted. During difficult times in our spiritual lives, we need some encouragement. David says in Psalm 23:4, "Yea though I walk through the valley of the shadow of death I will fear no evil . . ." Occasionally we will find ourselves in a situation where we feel ready to give up, as if we were at the point of death, figuratively or literally. However, just saying a prayer or having someone pray for us can comfort and revive us, restoring us to improved health.

Prayer also generates peace of mind, relieving us from the fear of death or condemnation and helping us triumph over evil forces. In addition, it gives us a boost of energy, strengthening the body and soul for another day's journey.

In Ephesians 6:10-12, Paul reminds us to be strong in the Lord: "For we wrestle not against flesh and blood, but against principalities, against powers, against the rulers of the darkness of this world, against spiritual wickedness in high places."

There are laws that govern this nation and rules and regulations that govern our workplaces. But there are also systems and powers in place that slowly but imperceptibly force us to divert from our godly principles. Through prayer, however, believers can neutralize some of these powers and make manifest the glory of God.

Physical problems have been resolved. Mark 6:41 tells us that Jesus held up five loaves of bread and two small fishes and prayed, after which He gave them to His disciples to feed the multitude. The results of prayer: more than five thousand men, women, and children ate until they were full.

In 1 Kings, chapter 18, we read that Elijah and his men prayed to the Lord God, who answered them by consuming the bullock with fire and drying up all the water, while Baal and his bullock remained untouched even after many prayers were offered.

The first chapter of 1 Samuel says that Hanna was unable to have children, and as a result she was mocked and provoked by her enemies. However, Hanna exercised her faith in prayer, crying and praying continuously to the Lord her God, asking Him for a son. In verse 20, we learn that her prayers were answered, bringing to an end all her doubts and fears. I can imagine her enemies must have felt defeated by Hanna's victory when she conceived and bore a son, Samuel.

In Acts, chapter 12, we read that King Herod had Peter thrown in prison. The church knelt down in prayer, and, as verse 5 states, that prayer was made without ceasing. As a result, an angel descended from heaven, smote Peter on his side, led him out of prison, and released him.

On numerous occasions, believers have testified that they were healed of an illness after someone prayed on their behalf. We've also been told of the power of prayer for expelling demonic spirits that tried to stifle human prosperity.

Financial dilemmas have been resolved. Believers have testified that after they prayed, their bills were taken care of so that they were free from their creditors. Four years after my husband and I bought our first home, we started having great financial strain. We were carrying a high balance on our credit cards, and our expenses were more than double our income. We tried cutting back on some things, but our debts kept escalating. I prayed daily to God for deliverance, never doubting that He would respond. After I refinanced the house for fear of losing it, God responded to my prayers by giving me the strength to work extra hours on the job. By accumulating additional income, I've been able to repay my debt gradually. This had to be, because God says in Genesis 3:19, "By the sweat of your face you will eat bread." Since then, things slowly have begun to improve. Today I give God thanks for answering my prayer, because we are now managing better.

Food has been provided to the hungry so that their bodies are nourished and strengthened for another day's journey.

The naked have been clothed and protected from the elements.

Shelter has been provided for the homeless, allowing them to bond together and be united.

All our daily needs have been supplied as a result of prayer.

God's servants on earth—His prophets, priests, evangelists, missionaries, even the least of His followers—have been actively promoting His works. What they have in common are their reports of great success, which could only have been achieved through continuous prayer.

They say that the family, who stays together, is the family who prays together. Prayer is the cord that connects and holds us to the supreme God of heaven. Therefore, for us to know our calling, fulfill our destiny, and feel that we are accomplishing our purpose on earth, we must live in continuous communication with God. With this as our main focus we can say, as Paul does in Romans 8:38, "For I am persuaded that neither death nor life, nor angels, nor principalities, nor powers, nor things present, nor things to come, nor height, nor depth, nor any other creature shall be able to separate us from the love of God."

Channels through which God responds

There are many channels through which God chooses to respond to the prayers of believers.

He sends angels to do the work, as He did when Peter was thrown into prison in Acts 12:7-10. In Psalm 34:7 David says, "The angel of the Lord encampeth round about them that fear him and delivereth them." Numerous individuals have testified about their encounters with angels, saying God sent angels to intervene on their behalf after prayer was offered.

He responds through other individuals. Sometimes when we face a difficult problem with no immediate solution, we can offer a prayer and God will send a complete stranger to address the situation, even though it was not made known to him or her. My neighbor, for example, was having great financial problems because illness had kept her out of work for a long time. At one point she was admitted to the hospital but returned home to recuperate, and I was led by the spirit to pray for her. I prayed that she would get better quickly, find employment soon, and recover financially, and that her family would experience peace. Two months later she called to thank me for the prayer and to let me know that her health had improved greatly, she now had a job, and things in her household were far better, too.

He responds through His word. God says in Mark 11:24, "Whatever you ask for in prayer, believe that you have received it and it will be yours." Whenever we pray, therefore, we should remind God of His promises and then claim our deliverance with authority. We should study the Bible, God's word, on a regular basis so that when we need an answer to our prayer, we can find it in the scriptures. There are verses there to address every concern we might encounter.

He responds through dreams. Many people have testified that God appeared to them in dreams or that their prayers were answered in the form of a dream. There's no doubt that Martin Luther King and his followers had a deep, intercessory prayer before each of his congregational speeches. In his greatest and most famous speech, he said to the crowd "I have a dream that one day this nation will rise up and live out the true meaning of its creed . . . that all men are created equal . . . that my four children will one day live in a nation where they will not be judged by the color of their skin but by the content of their character".

He responds through circumstances. I spent months driving around in a van that was badly damaged on the bumper and front end. Because the bumper and headlight had to be replaced entirely and fixing the dents would require costly bodywork, I lacked the funds to take the van to the body shop. However, when I took it to the dealership for regular servicing, the mechanic accidentally crashed the vehicle, causing greater damage to the already affected areas. This was an answered prayer for me, because the dealership had to fix their damage, which included mine. As a result, my cost for repairs was minimal, an amount that I could actually afford.

Finally, we read in Mark, chapter 9, that Jesus expelled a mute and deaf spirit from a young boy. When the disciples asked Jesus why they hadn't been able to cast out the spirit, Jesus reminded them that it could only be accomplished with prayer and fasting. Therefore, in order for us to survive and be victorious over all the problems in life, we must pray daily, all year long. Every believer should use the tool of prayer as the master key for solving every difficulty in life, large or small.

Individual Prayers

These prayers can be used as a guide when praying for different concerns in your daily life. They have worked for me in various situations when I faced problems or challenges.

I like finding the appropriate prayer for providing strength in my time of need. It is like placing a telephone call to headquarters—I can place a special order while also pulling power from my spiritual reservoir.

The Lord's Prayer

Some Christians are satisfied repeating just the Lord's Prayer. Others prefer to construct their own prayer that relates to their present feelings or emotions and expresses their thoughts. Then, at the conclusion of their own prayer, they might choose to recite the Lord's Prayer.

> *Our Father which art in heaven,*
> *hallowed be thy name.*
> *Thy kingdom come.*
> *thy will be done*
> *in earth, as it is in heaven.*
> *Give us this day our daily bread.*
> *And forgive us our debts,*
> *as we forgive our debtors.*
> *And lead us not into temptation,*
> *but deliver us from evil:*
> *for thine is the kingdom, and the power, and the glory, for*
> *ever. Amen.*

Dear Lord

*Dear Lord, savior divine, I present myself before you this
moment.
I acknowledge that you are omnipresent and
your glory permeates the whole earth.
Your goodness and your mercies have no end.
Your divinity is above and beyond human comprehension;
yet, Lord, you avail yourself for a base thing like me.
Thanks for the opportunity to associate myself with you.
You told us that we are your children and the sheep of your
pasture.
Today we ask for forgiveness of sins.
So help us to forgive our brothers and sisters.
Then help us to love and serve you as dear children of God.
Help us to love our neighbors and live peacefully with one another.
Supply our daily needs as you have promised.
Make all our undertakings prosperous, as we undertake them
for the glorification of your name.
Bless us spiritually, physically, and financially.
Grant us wisdom, knowledge, understanding, and the power
to prevail against every force that rises and tries to stifle our
opportunities toward success.
Then help us to run with the torch of salvation until the race
is over.
In your great name, Lord, I pray.
Amen.*

Prayer for the Home

The home can be the foundation for the development of either good or evil. A home that is to neutralize evil and produce blessings and prosperity for future generations should be fully equipped with the tool of prayer, which is used on a daily basis.

Below is an example of a prayer which could be used as a guideline when praying for the home.

Bless this home, dear Lord,
as it provides all the necessities that enable our family to stay
together willingly for ten, twenty, thirty years, or more.
Provide the joy and comfort, the warmth and safety,
the spirit of welcome and love for your people as they enter
through these doors.
Send a guarding spirit to occupy every room.
Let all empty space be filled with your love
as the radiance of your presence illuminates every area.
Let there be joyful sounds of laughter as children play within
the comfort of these walls.
Let peace and love reign in the heart of everyone who shelters
within these walls.
Let all utility bills be paid in full and on time.
And Lord, protect this home from being burglarized by those
who refuse to work honestly for their daily bread.
Shelter this home from all natural and man-made disasters,
and let it be a foretaste of heaven
for all who enter and exit through these doors.
In your holy name I pray.
Amen.

Prayer for the Family

Today's family is targeted by the forces of evil on a daily basis. These forces use the weapon of separation to destroy and nullify the foundation of the family. As a means of fighting back, families must pray daily for love and peace to abide within them.

Below is an example of a prayer for the family.

*Lord, here we are before you: Mom and Dad, brother and sister,
and then here's Rex, our little pet.
We are a family standing before you collectively, but we seek
individual blessings from you.
In this our family, Lord, we pray for love, peace, and
understanding.
You created everyone differently,
so we need wisdom to deal fairly and without bias with each other.
Knit us together with cord that is unbreakable.
Provide for the children; let them grow and adopt good morals
and true Christian principles.
Bless Mom and Dad so their marriage will be forever and
filled with love and forgiveness.
Give them strength to work honestly for every day's needs.
Take care of our pet, whether it is a mammal, bird, or fish.
Let us live in harmony with nature, and
Lord, let this family be the perfect example of what you
intended a family to be.
And bless all the other families of the earth as we all unite
and live in harmony for the perfection of your will.
In your holy name, Lord, I pray.
Amen.*

Prayer for My Education

Knowledge has become the most powerful tool we can have. If knowledge is not used wisely, however, it can cause great problems in society. Everyone who attends school does so with the anticipation of achieving an education that will allow him to live a good and dignified lifestyle. But we must be very careful in our choice of studies, because some knowledge could lead to our downfall.

It is a wise thing to pray earnestly that our education will have a positive impact on us and our environment. Below is an example which could be used when praying for your education.

Dear Lord, I enter this schoolroom today
with the intention to achieve a good education.
I pray that you let my brain be receptive to the good and
sound knowledge that is being offered.
Your word reminds us to study to show ourselves worthy of you.
Help us, your children, to learn whatever is necessary and
appropriate
so that we can apply our knowledge to build a successful and
safe community.
Teach us, Lord, to adopt the language of love and forgiveness.
Give us the wisdom to judge between good and evil,
and help us understand that the fear of you, Lord, is the
beginning of all wisdom.
Inspire our teachers to impart their wisdom and knowledge to us.
Bless them with patience, gentleness, and endurance
as they help mold us into the perfect characters you intended
us to be.
Thank you, Lord, for hearing this prayer.
In your holy name I pray.
Amen.

Prayer for the Sick

Humans have long been plagued by diseases that pose a great challenge to physicians. However, illness poses no problem to Almighty God, the greatest physician. Within Him lies the source to eradicate all form of sickness. For this resource to be activated, humans must do two things: believe in His heavenly power and ask for His intervention. Below is an example of a prayer that could be used when seeking God's intervention.

Jesus, love divine, God, my savior and friend,
I come before you this day in the spirit of humility,
knowing that within you lies the source of all our needs.
Lord, you are the greatest physician who heals body and soul.
This day, dear Lord, I present my disease-stricken body before
you for full restoration.
Lord, I am weak; please restore strength to my bones.
My muscles cry out under daily, excruciating pain.
Please reach to the root of the pain and neutralize those nerves.
My organ systems have become confused and have started to
malfunction
from interference by infectious diseases.
I pray now that you will heal my body from all illness.
Rebuke schizophrenia and depression,
which plague the mind.
Eradicate cancer, leukemia, and myeloma,
which infest the cells.
Sluice out diabetes, oh Lord! It's too sweet for my blood.
Then, Lord, there are arthritis, bronchitis, and meningitis,
glaucoma and cataracts.
And don't forget heart attack and stroke.

Then there are other afflictions that I have not mentioned,
but you know them all.
Please rid my body of all disease and allow me to be a
testimony of your true healing power.
In your holy name I pray.
Amen.

Prayer for Prosperity

It is the will of God that man prosper and be in good health. Psalm 112:1-3 states that wealth and riches shall be in the house of the man who fears the Lord and delights in his commandments. It is therefore biblically correct for one to pray for health, wealth, and prosperity.

Below is an example of a prayer for prosperity.

Jesus, king of kings, lord of lords, and savior of the world, we come before you this day empty-handed but with the assurance that all our needs will be met.
You told us in your word that if we abide in you and your word abides in us,
we might ask what we will and it shall be granted.
Today we pray for prosperity in every aspect of our lives, as we sink our roots deep down and draw from the living source.
We claim prosperity in our finances, that our pockets shall be filled and running over.
We claim prosperity in our business endeavors, that they will grow and flourish.
Let there be great demand for our products and services, that there will be no need for downsizing or closure.
We claim prosperity in our jobs that we can perform them with good spirit and our service will be fairly rewarded.
We claim prosperity for our families that love will bind us together and none of us shall be cheated by untimely death.
We claim prosperity for our children, that they will be leaders and not followers.
We claim prosperity for your people that they will be like trees that flourish on the riverbanks.

*Peace and contentment, sunshine and rain shall pour down
from heaven on your children,
Now and forever.
Amen.*

Prayer for the Children

Children are God's heritage, so they deserve to grow, mature, and fulfill their God-given abilities. We should pray for our children daily so they will respect the presence of God and His leadership in their lives.

Dear Lord, we pray for your blessings on all the children of the world.
Red, yellow, black, or white, all are precious in your sight.
Bless them as they grow and change from stage to stage.
Bless them with good grades; help them receive an excellent education.
Let them grow and choose respectable careers with excellent wages.
Give them the qualities of a good leader or a loving teacher, for they are the world changers of tomorrow.
Let everywhere they go and everything they touch be transformed, producing an abundance of blessing.
Give them good health and a long life.
But most of all let them never forget that you are the source of all their achievements and that all glory belongs to you as you shower them with an abundance of blessings.
In your holy name we pray.
Amen

Workplace Prayer

Most employees are faced with diverse challenges in today's workplace. The pressures created by these challenges can cause many employees to become frustrated beyond their powers of resistance. Genesis 3:19 states that "in the sweat of thy face shall thou eat bread." Therefore in order to survive in the work force, we must cultivate and maintain good work ethics. We can do this by offering daily prayers for wisdom, strength, and a positive attitude as we enter and exit the workplace. Below is an example of such a workplace prayer.

Dear Lord, it's another day and I ask you to give me strength,
the strength to enter this workplace once more.
My boss comes around, Lord, with the rod of oppression,
but forgive him, because he's been driven with the rod of
oppression, also.
At times I am so furious, Lord, that I want to grab my bag
and escape to the comfort of my home.
But thank you for the still, small voice that reminds me that
by the sweat of my brow I shall eat bread.
Lord, today I pray for the wisdom to work skillfully on the job.
I pray for the knowledge to understand and do what is
expected of me within my scope of training.
I pray for the understanding to discern why I have been
placed in this position.
I pray for the patience to bear with the differences among my
fellow workers.
I pray for unity among workers and staff,
and I ask that you give everyone a positive attitude,
a team spirit,
and the desire to work and make the world a better place.
Amen.

A Kitchen Prayer

A sanctuary is a place where the soul receives food for spiritual growth. The kitchen is a sanctuary that contains the source for physical growth. In order to have supplies in abundance so that the storeroom never goes empty, we should pray specifically for that blessing.

Below is an example of a kitchen prayer.

Dear Lord, thank you for this day.
I'm here in my kitchen to prepare a nutritious, tasty, and colorful meal.
Fill this kitchen with the sweet aromas of fresh herbs, spices, and oil.
Restock the fridge with fresh fruits and vegetables and an abundance of milk.
My storage basket or pantry, Lord, should never be empty, for your angel might stop by someday, and he would be very disappointed if there were not enough food and milk and honey.
Lord, let the knives, forks, and spoons sing for joy as they serve the hungry mouth.
Let the plates, pots, and pans be delighted to serve up some mouth-watering meals.
Lord, give me strength daily to perform the duties of a good home chef.
And let this, my kitchen, be a supplier for the hungry,
A well of water for the thirsty,
and a container for the main ingredients that hold a loving family together.
In your great name, Lord, I pray.
Amen.

Mealtime Prayer

Jesus established a perfect example of mealtime prayer when he held up five loaves of bread and two fried fishes and gave thanks for them. For this reason, believers have embraced the concept of giving thanks for all meals on a daily basis.

Below is one example of mealtime prayer.

Good and bounteous is your love, oh God,
as we experience it in this table laden with appetizing food
and beverages.
There are fruits and vegetables in different sizes, shapes, and
colors;
meat and fish, seasoned and cooked with lots of spices and herbs;
freshly prepared staples accompanied by hot, steaming gravy;
and then drink in abundance—and Lord, you provided them all.
Bless and sanctify every dish as we partake of it.
Let this meal nourish and strengthen our bodies
as we dive in with great delight.
Bless those who prepared it willingly and with love.
Refill their pantries, which they emptied out to feed these
hungry hearts.
And let the spirit of sharing continue among your people,
now and forever.
In your great name I pray.
Amen.

A Bathroom Prayer

"In everything give thanks: for this is the will of God in Christ Jesus concerning you." (1 Thess. 5:18). We are created so that whatever enters through the mouth has to exit the body in some form. The bathroom, therefore, is a small but import part of the home, as it is within this room that the family finds comfort in relieving the waste from the body, whether through elimination or showering. Then it's time to dress and beautify the body, as reflected in the mirror on the wall. These are some of the great reasons why every household should adopt the practice of having a bathroom prayer.

Below is an example.

Gentle Jesus, love divine,
I clasp my hands and bow my head to you this day
as I sit on this device.
I take comfort in relieving the waste from my body.
Thank you, Lord, for the elimination system,
a system that works so well to give me comfort when I feel I've
got to go right now.
Thank you for that shower, which gives me such a refreshing
feeling each time I lather up and wash away hours of perspiration,
And not to mention that golden mirror on the wall,
which allows me to see how beautiful God made me.
Thank you, Lord, for the undisturbed peace that I feel
each time I close the bathroom door and sit on that bowl,
relaxing with the Bible or the newspaper and meditating on you.
Thank you, Lord, for the satisfaction that I feel
each time I enter and exit that bathroom.
Amen.

Baby's Dedication Prayer

The baby dedication has been a tradition since biblical times. Luke, chapter 2, tells us that Simeon took the baby Jesus in his arms and blessed God. This same ritual has been practiced down throughout the years, and even today, parents consider this a vital tradition in the first stage of a child's life. Below is an example of a baby dedication prayer.

Gentle Jesus, meek and mild,
thank you for your powers that you have demonstrated in this, your little child.
Lord, you took nine months to fully fashion this earthly angel in his mother's womb,
and now you present him to us to be loved and cared for.
As we hold him in our arms and look in his eyes,
he reminds us of how great you are.
Today we dedicate him to your divine will.
Spread a rainbow of protection around this, your child.
Grant him perfect health as he grows and matures into adulthood.
Give him a personality as pleasant as the rising sun and calm as the morning dew.
Help him to grow healthy, make good judgments, and exercise wisdom in every aspect of his life.
Let him be an instrument of your divine will as your glory shines all around him.
Grant him perfect peace all the days of his life.
And may your purpose be perfected through him, now and forever.
Amen.

A Child's Prayer

"Train up a child in the way he should go and when he is old he will not depart from it" (Prov. 22:6). It is of great importance that a child learns the principles of prayer from an early stage. By so doing, the child will grow up to appreciate the reasons for and benefits of saying a prayer in reverence to God.

Below is an example of a child's prayer.

Heavenly Father, I come into your holy presence this day to
acknowledge you as my father and friend.
Today I give you thanks for your loving care and ask for
continued guidance through life's journey.
Tonight as I viewed the sky, I saw a bright star,
a star that stood out for its beauty and radiance.
I claim this star to be mine tonight as I ask you to transform
my life into such a radiant star.
Take my hands and feet as they practice and prepare to face
the challenges of each new day.
Take my eyes and ears; let them see and hear only the
harmonious beauty of your world.
Take my voice as I tune it to sing praises to you.
Take my whole being as I try to condition it to your will.
And may your love be portrayed in this little star
as I meditate on thee
now and forever.
Amen.

Prayer of a Mother

*Lord, I come before your presence this moment to address all
my cares and concerns.*
I thank you, first, for entrusting motherhood to me.
You caused me to bring forth children, your heritage.
*You created in me love, patience, and all the qualities
required to grow and nurture children*
*Then you charged me to train up the child in the way he should
go so that when he is old he will not depart from these principles.*
*Lord, I carried out these duties through good times and bad
times, through sorrow and pain.*
*There were times, Lord, when I felt that I had not done enough.
But Lord, please forgive my insufficiency.*
*Now that my children have grown and become parents themselves,
guide them so they will do a good job with their own children.*
*Now that I have spent my many years gathering wisdom
through experience, allow me to be an additional light in
their darkest moments.*
*Now that my skin is wrinkled and sags from many years of
caring and hurting,*
*I pray that my spirit of love, kindness, and compassion will be
manifest in my children and their children, now and forever.*
Amen.

Prayer of a Father

Good gracious, Lord! When did I grow up to become an adult?
It seems as if it was just yesterday that I was a boy;
now I am a man, and you've entrusted upon me fatherhood.
Lord, to be a father is one heck of a task.
Listen, Lord—I cannot do this without your help.
You made me to be strong and courageous,
yet I become weak and helpless when the baby cries.
You made me to become the breadwinner of the family,
yet I am immature when it comes to holding a bottle to feed
the little one.
You created a rough and fearless personality in me;
now I'm wondering how I should interact with my teenage
daughter.
Will my grown daughter be happy to say "I do" to some
stranger because her father has lived and set a good example?
Will my grown son be satisfied that I was a good role model
for him?
Lord, all these concerns trouble me greatly.
I need your help now, Lord, as I ponder these thoughts.
Now help me to be that strong, loving, and nurturing father
you intended me to be,
as I enter into your holy presence.
Amen.

Prayer for My Country

Beautiful country, land of sunshine, rain, and snow—
Lord, you created this country through your fathomless
wisdom, with me in mind.
Today, Lord, I'm asking for your blessing on this, my country,
a land which has now become my home and a home for many
others who are called by your name.
Bless this country with fertile soil to produce an abundance of
fruits, vegetables, and grains.
Bless this country with natural resources to fulfill the need of
every individual.
Provide all citizens with gainful opportunities to labor
honestly for their daily bread.
Bless the leaders with wisdom from above, and let peace,
love, and contentment rain down on your people, big, small,
black, or white.
Prevent all man-made and natural disasters form destroying
that which has been accomplished and cause this, my country,
to be a replica of heaven on earth, where your glory will be
seen in the rising sun and your comfort in the night sky.
Blessings and prosperity shall reign now and always.
In your holy name I pray.
Amen.

Prayer for Rulers and Leaders

All leaders have great responsibilities entrusted to them according to the measure of their God-given talent. Usually their followers consist of many different personalities—some are well-mannered, while others display a posse mentality, which can become a challenge even to the greatest leader. Because of these challenges, and because a leader is ultimately responsible for the growth, failure, or success of his team, Paul encourages us in 1 Timothy, chapter 2, to pray for kings and all those in authority. Below is an example that can be followed when praying for leaders and rulers.

Heavenly Father, you are the God of our salvation,
the judge of our souls, the ruler of heaven and earth.
Today we acknowledge your power as the highest.
All powers and authority are subject to your divine ruling.
Lord, we come before you today on behalf of all leaders in the
secular world and the spiritual realm.
We pray for all rulers, councilors, judges, decision makers, law
enforcement officers, managers, and bosses in all places.
We pray for all heads of government as they gather to make
decisions for the edification of your people.
We pray that the laws they implement will be designed to
relieve the oppression of your people.
We pray for leaders who recognize and believe in your divinity.
We pray for leaders who denounce you as Lord of the universe;
may you forgive their lack of spiritual wisdom.
We pray for church leaders; they are the Moses and Joshuas
of today.
We pray for wisdom, knowledge, understanding, strength, and
good health for every individual who holds a
leadership position.

We present them all collectively to your care,
but Lord, we pray that your love and mercy will forever be
on them individually, now and always.
Amen.

Prayer for My Husband

Husbands are encouraged to love their wives even as God loves the church. A wife should be submissive but pray earnestly for her husband. If a wife is devoted to prayer, certainly this will result in her husband leading a more effective family life. In turn, their children will adopt healthier lifestyles with Christian morals, longer-lasting marriages, financial responsibility, and love and harmony in the home.

Below is an example of a prayer for the husband.

Lord, from your measureless love you created man,
and you fashioned him after your measureless beauty.
From his side you chose to create woman as his wife.
Today I praise you for your love and thank you for my husband.
Thank you for his role—to love, to cherish, and to be the
breadwinner of the family.
Give him strength as he goes from day to day, doing his job to
secure our livelihood.
Give him the wisdom to mediate fairly when his family needs
his intervention.
Give him love to share unconditionally when his family seems
to fall short.
Give him the knowledge to recognize all that makes up a
loving and prosperous family.
Give him the understanding to know when to be quiet and
listen to the simplest of conversations.
Give him the will to act as the head of his family but to be
submissive to your divine leading.
Help him exhibit pure and unconditional love for his wife,
who is bone of his bones and flesh of his flesh.

Veronica O' Connor

I pray for blessings and prosperity in all his undertakings, and may power, valor, and strength be upon him all the days of his life.
Amen.

Prayer for My Wife

They say that behind every successful man is a good woman. Ephesians 5:25 admonishes husbands to love their wives even as Christ loves the church. Wives are the backbone of the family, attending to the simplest but most essential details in life. For these and other reasons mentioned in the prayer below, husbands should engage in deep intercessory prayer for their wives.

Below is a prayer that husbands can use as a guideline when praying for their wives.

*Blessed Jesus, savior and Lord, today I come before you on
behalf of my wife.
Lord, you created woman as man's helpmeet, and you created
man to be the head of the family.
Today, Lord, I give you thanks for my wife.
She provides me with unconditional love and affection,
without which I would be incomplete.
She prepares my meals with such love and care that sometimes
it's hard to resist the carbs.
She takes care of my laundry without even asking for
servant's pay.
She cleans and decorates the house so that even angels would
feel welcome to enter there.
She willingly bears my children, one after the other, without
asking compensation for the cost of labor.
Lord, she makes me very proud.
So today I ask you to bless her in a very special way.
Forgive her when she snaps angrily at my simplest mistake.
Keep her calm and at peace when her hormones are raging.
Satisfy her every need so that she is in want of nothing.*

Keep her sweet, glowing, and beautiful every day,
and bind our love together now and for always.
In your holy name I pray.
Amen.

Prayer of Commitment

God created me as an instrument of His love. In spite of His seal on my life, I've still had many deeply challenging moments—challenging enough for me to consider cancelling my existence on earth. After I regained my composure, however, I realized that entry into heaven requires deep, faithful commitment and lots of self-sacrifice.

Below is a sample prayer vowing my commitment to God.

Holy Father, today I come to you in the name of Jesus Christ.
I worship and praise you as Lord and king of my life.
I am your creation; therefore I commit my whole being as an instrument of your praise.
I commit my feet to you as they tread the pathway to present you to the lost and dying.
I commit my hands to you as they perform good deeds to satisfy and bring comfort to the needy.
I commit my tongue to you to be used as a messenger of good news.
I commit my eyes to you so that I can see the enemy from afar, but also, that I can see the good and upright in someone else.
I commit my ears to you; let me hear the cry of the helpless and hear when you speak in that still, small voice.
I commit my nose to you; let me smell the sweet fragrance of roses and daffodils, for they are reflections of your handiwork.
I commit my whole self to you to be used as a vessel of honor in your service.
Now I commit my commitment into your care.
Help me to fulfill my duties with excellence, now and forever.
Amen.

The Night's Prayer

We wake up each morning with the hope that we will be able accomplish the day's tasks and be free from physical, emotional, or spiritual pain; however, this is not always possible. Then, at the end of the day when we settle down to sleep, we become vulnerable to the elements of darkness. As children of God, it is appropriate for us to give thanks for accomplishing the day's activities and then ask for His protection throughout the night.

Below is an example of this type of prayer.

Dear Lord Jesus, the day is over, and the night has just begun.
We thank you for what we have accomplished over the past hours.
As we meditate on you now,
Lord we seek your protection throughout the night.
We realize that as we sleep, we are removed from consciousness
and become open to the powers of darkness.
Please form a ring of protection around us as we sleep and
remove all negative forces from around us.
Disperse all powers of darkness and lighten the atmosphere as
we sleep beneath your wings.
Restore and rebuild all our damaged and worn-out cells.
Rejuvenate our bodies and give strength to our weak bones,
so that when we awake in the morning, our body, mind, and
spirit will be equipped and ready to face the challenges of
another new day.
Thanks for hearing this prayer
as we settle in your holy presence.
Amen.

The Day's Prayer

This is the day that the Lord has made;
I will rejoice and be glad there in.
Today, Lord, I ask for another portion of your mercies as I
take life one day at a time.
Lord, today has just begun, and within it lays the unknown.
We pray that you will go before us and lead us in green
pastures all the days of our lives.
Today we pray for health, wealth, and a strong desire for your
will.
Give us this day, Lord, our daily bread as we labor honestly by
the sweat of our brow.
Grant us peace and contentment, and bless your children
so that at the end of the day, your will will beaccomplish in
earth as it is in heaven, now and forever.
Amen.

A Sinner's Prayer

To be accepted into the kingdom of God, we must recognize and accept that we are sinners and believe that forgiveness can be accomplished only through Jesus Christ Himself. When we fail in our efforts and see the need to make a spiritual recommitment, we can use this prayer as a guideline, after which a spiritual leader should be contacted for further support.

Jesus, my creator and the savior of the world,
I first give you thanks for creating me in your own image and
after your own likeness.
You said that the whole duty of man is to serve you and keep
your commandments.
I come before you, Lord, to acknowledge that I am a sinner
who needs to be to be forgiven of my sins and be saved.
I have strayed far from your presence
and realize that I am nothing without you.
I cannot survive and fulfill my purpose without you.
So, Lord, I now give my life completely to you.
Forgive me of all my sins.
Cleanse my heart and soul with your precious blood,
and accept me into your kingdom once more,
so that I can experience sweet fellowship with your divineness.
In your holy name I pray.
Amen.

Prayer of a Troubled Soul

There are times when life's burdens seem unbearable and life's problems seem never-ending, causing the soul to cry out in deep desperation. However, we very often forget that Christ, our source of strength, is readily available to be tapped.

Below is an example of a prayer that can be used when we are in a desperate situation and our faith is challenged by the powers that be.

Oh Lord, my God and my redeemer,
I had almost forgotten that you are my only source,
ready to be tapped.
Lord, for a little while I was carried away by my oppressors.
I wondered,
Lord, how the numbers increased who trouble me,
how their numbers increased who rise up against me.
They said to my soul, "There is no help for you in God."
Lord, when shall I rise up out of the mire?
When shall my enemies be defeated and cease plotting against
my soul?
Today, Lord, I feel that I've reached the Red Sea of my sorrows.
Behind me bellows a desperate tsunami, before me the desert
seems impassable,
and above me the darkness of the night hovers.
Jesus, son of God, I wait in desperation for your help
as I now surrender to the only God I know.
May your will be accomplished in me,
may your glory and strength be made manifest
before the eyes of all men, now and forever.
In your holy name I pray.
Amen.

Prayer to Defeat the Enemy

This prayer can be used when the enemy tries to attack with the weapons of fear, failure, and rejection.

The Lord is my shepherd; I shall not fail.
Though the devices of the wicked stretch out against me,
they will not prosper,
for Jehovah is my source, and in Him will I be confident.
Though the enemy gathers around me like an army,
the Lord God shall scatter them like feathers in the wind.
They will be defeated, as God's people shall flourish and
prosper in the presence of the ungodly.
For Jehovah is my rod and staff,
which shall comfort me all the days of my life,
and I will praise him forever and ever.
Amen.

Prayer of Thanksgiving

As hard as we work and as much as we try to condition ourselves to good and upright living, we cannot prosper without the intervention of God. Wisdom, knowledge, and understanding are engraved on our DNA by God Himself and then made manifest in our actions as we grow and mature. As a result, it is necessary that we find time to give thanks regularly for the things that benefit us in our daily lives. Below is an example of a thanksgiving prayer.

Father, we thank you for this, another day; we shall rejoice and be glad therein.
Thank you for waking us today.
We awoke to your glory, the brightness of the dawn, and the freshness of a new day,
with the hum of insects and the chirping of birds in the air.
Father, we are still in the comfort of our homes,
where we feel safe and secure and where an appetizing meal is prepared every day to feed some hungry mouth.
For these blessings and many more, dear Lord, we thank you.
We thank you for our families, who love and forgive us unconditionally.
We thank you for our jobs, providing us the opportunity to earn a salary, which helps to take care of living expenses.
Then, Lord, we thank you for the fruitfulness of Mother Earth, who supplies nutrients to every plant
and holds all structures, great and small, in the palm of her hand.
No wonder you chose a portion of earth to create this body of mine, which hosts your precious breath.
We thank you for all plants, animals, birds, and creatures of the sea, great and small;
you gave them all to us as a source of food for the body.

We thank you for the elements of the air,
the sun, moon, and stars, even the very wind.
Scientists can testify to their rich properties, how greatly they
complement the human race.
We thank you for wisdom, knowledge, and understanding.
How could we survive if we were not knowledgeable of the
things surrounding us?
Lord, thanks and praise shall continually be on our lips,
our hearts shall be lifted up, and our spirits shall be in
submission to your rich blessings, now and forever.
Amen.

End of Life Prayer

As a health professional, I have worked among hundreds of clients during their final days of life. I've noticed that some became restless and anxious, others calm and peaceful, and still others withdrawn and fearful of the unknown. Usually, believers in Christ exhibit a pleasant and welcoming countenance as they patiently await the transition from life to death.

Below is an example of a prayer that can be used during the special moment when someone is preparing to exit his or her earthly body.

Heavenly host, I welcome your presence around me just now.
Here I am, near the end of my journey,
just waiting to hear "Come home."
Lord, I hope that I achieved my earthly purpose well.
I hope that I was a light in someone's darkness,
a source of strength to some weak links,
a friend to the unfriendly,
and an archive of source to the seekers.
Here I patiently await your next move
as I take this opportunity to examine my soul once more.
I pray for forgiveness of my sins,
sins that I knowingly committed
and sins that I've committed unaware.
Remove the nervousness and fear that stand between me
and you just now.
Replace them with joy and assurance that the angels will
escort my soul into the comfort of your hands
to begin life anew in your glorious kingdom.
In the name of Jesus Christ I pray.
Amen.

Prayer at the Graveside

When we reach the end of our earthly existence, our body and our soul return to their respective resting places. Usually the officiating minister prays a last prayer at the graveside, giving thanks for the beloved, for his or her accomplishments, and for the quality of life that he or she was able to enjoy.

Below is an example of a prayer offered for someone who has dedicated his life to the service of God.

Almighty God, our Lord and savior,
we gather before you this day
to commit our dear loved one back to you.
We thank you for his earthly life,
a life that was filled with challenges.
Lots of prizes and surprises,
joys and sorrows, grief and pain,
successes here and failures there,
riches and poverty—
all these came in one package, but Lord, you helped him all
the way through.
Since his earthly existence has now come to an end
and earth now reclaims his body,
heaven rejoices and welcomes his soul.
We thank you, Lord, and we praise you for everything
as we close this chapter in the life of our beloved
and commit his body back to the earth and his spirit and
soul into your hands.
Through your holy name we pray.
Amen.

References

Gen. 4:26

> And to Seth, to him also there was born a son; and he called his name Enos: then began men to call upon the name of the Lord.

Matt. 6:7

> But when ye pray, use not vain repetitions, as the heathen do; for they think that they shall be heard for their much speaking.

Zech. 13:9

> They shall call on my name and I will hear them; I will say it is my people and they shall say the Lord is my God.

John 15:7

> If ye abide in me and my words abide in you, ye shall ask what ye will and it shall be done unto you.

Matt. 26:41

> Watch and prey that ye enter not into temptation.

Matt. 18:1

And he spake a parable unto them to this end, that men ought always to pray and not to faint.

Eph. 6:18

Praying always with all prayer and supplication in the spirit, and watching therefore with all perseverance and supplication for all saints.

Matt. 7:7

Ask, and it shall be given you; seek, and ye shall find; knock, and it shall be opened unto you.

1 Tim. 2:8

I will therefore that men pray everywhere lifting up holy hands without wrath and doubting.

James 5:16

Confess your faults one to another and pray one for another that he may be healed. The effective fervent prayer of a righteous man availeth much.

Ps. 34:17

The righteous cry and the Lord heareth and delivereth them out of all their troubles.

Ps. 91:15

He shall call upon me, and I will answer him; I will be with him in trouble; I will deliver him and honor him.

Ps. 18:6

In my distress I called upon the Lord and cried unto my God; he heard my voice out of his temple and my cry came before him, even into his ears.

Ps. 55:1

Give ear to my prayer, O God and hide not thyself from my supplication.

Prov. 15:29

The Lord is far from the wicked but he heareth the prayer of the righteous.

Author Profile

Veronica O'Connor was born in Point Hill, Jamaica, on February 2, 1958.

She accepted Jesus Christ in her life at the age of twelve. She taught at the Point Hill Basic School for twelve years and then taught for an additional two years at the primary school, after which she immigrated to Toronto, Canada. In Canada she continued to further her education and switched from teaching to enter the health field, where she presently works as a registered practical nurse. Veronica continued to explore her God-given talent, and in 2006 she wrote and published a cookbook, *Veronica's Caribbean Dishes*. As her spiritual desire became more intense, she saw the need to write this book, *Prayer or Communication with God*.

Because Veronica has had many positive experiences as a result of prayer and through her strong and continued faith in God, she felt the urge to share some of them with others. She hopes that the daily use of and meditation on the contents of this book will be life-changing for readers.